Praise for *Again*

Charles Douthat's beautiful new book of poems, *Again*, is dedicated to the proposition that the family pool has no shallow end, and that there's nothing ordinary about the most ordinary of attachments, of child to parent, parent to child, or sibling to sibling. In an elegantly unadorned yet lyrical plain style, free of cant or fakery, Douthat recreates the lost and troubled members of his childhood family so vividly that we feel not so much the presence of the past as the heart wrenching pastness of the past, in all its unresolved and unresolvable complexity. This is a book impossible not to love.

Alan Shapiro, author of *Night of the Republic*

Elegiac, edged with humor and grace, Charles Douthat's *Again* offers a sweeping vista of a California where "[s]omewhere birds were thinking / of singing" and family dead speak again through memory. In these poems, you'll find yourself in rooms so vivid you can touch their brass door-keys and feel the light on your own face. Douthat's poems meditate on leaving, on last encounters — yet offer spaces of possibility and renewal. "Soon each must let go the other's hand," one speaker says. Liminal, voiced by a mother, a father, a sister, the poems of *Again* show us a mind recounting the whole of a person, of a family which for all its "hungers, angers and joys" was loved.

Tyler Mills, author of *Hawk Parable*

This is the book of poetry one prays for, rarely gets.

Nancy Fitz-Hugh Meneely, author of *Letter from Italy, 1944*

Charles Douthat mines a deep vein of the meditative lyric that runs adjacent to the later poems of Wallace Stevens. With a soulful, intelligent sustenato of memory and meaning, Douthat's *Again* is more fully narrative, and more intimate than late Stevens. His book's four sections sift through stories of mother and father, sister and brother, all of them rendered in retrospect now, in living again, where the mundane everyday gains deeper resonance, tenderness, and sorrow. Douthat writes of living and dying, poem by poem, recalling the troubled (sometimes addicted) lives of a family, reaching in his final section a profound opening-out both of style and vista where — in memory and poetry's paradox — there is "so much life afterwards."

David Baker, author of *Swift, New and Selected Poems*

This is a book about memory and second-thoughts. The original experience is presented in clear detail, but upon recollection, a different reality is shaken loose. It's the process of shaking loose the deeper meanings of the originating moment that gives these poems their movement and their emotional force. Nothing is ever as we once experienced it or thought of it — the deeper dive that art requires, always leads us to a new understanding, perhaps one we can barely apprehend, yet receive it as a loving and life-giving spark. Each poem in this book is a sustaining spark, despite the grief and loss they overcome. I'm glad to have these sputters and glimpses of vision in our world. *Again* is a book of clarity and serious power, wrought from long life and its restraints.

Maurice Manning, author of *The Common Man*

Lorca said "the artist is one who takes the world into the self, sifts it through the self, and then gives it back to the world." When an artist accomplishes that sifting for us — as Charles Douthat has in his new book — and does it with craft, tenderness and genuine compassion, we receive "the world" made luminous, the world redeemed. In *Again,* Douthat gives us poems that are morally and spiritually essential, that convey the very breath of life.

Gray Jacobik, author of *The Banquet, New and Selected Poems*

Again

Again Charles Douthat

ed.
UNBOUND EDITION PRESS
Atlanta

FIRST EDITION

Printed in the United States of America

LIBRARY OF CONGRESS RECORD

Name: Douthat, Charles , 1950 — author.
Title: Last Day on Earth in the Eternal City / Angie Estes.
Edition: First edition.
Published: Atlanta : Unbound Edition Press, 2025.

LCCN: 2024946029
LCCN Permalink: https://lccn.loc.gov/2024946029
ISBN: 979-8-9906141-8-5 (fine softcover)

Designed by Eleanor Safe and Joseph Floresca
Printed by Bookmobile, Minneapolis, MN
Distributed by Itasca Books

123456789

Unbound Edition Press
1270 Caroline Street, Suite D120
Box 448
Atlanta, GA 30307

For my family.

Contents

2. LATER

3. THEN

4. AFTER

Again

We have begun to say good bye
To each other
And cannot say it

GEORGE OPPEN

Mercy

And afterwards, furnaced by midday Roman heat

and tired steps away from St. Peters and the Pope's
golf-cart ride through the square's adoring crowd,
we were resting within an ancient arched portico

when the two white pigeons winged down, settling
on t-shirted shoulders of our eight-year-old daughter.
Cautiously — half-delighted, half-frightened — she

raised arms and the birds stepped along, perching
finally on uplifted hands. Gravely Jeanne looked at
us then, with a spirit that made us feel mysteriously

taller, younger, fortunate, cared for ... whatever word
best describes that which we search restless worlds for,
pry open resentful hearts for, drop to bended knees for,

but which seems to come only as those pigeons came.
When we're worn. When we've all but given up on
making more of our day or the year or ourselves,

having lost faith that such finery will ever be bestowed
on us again. Yet isn't that how it arrives? Unbidden
and glossed so abundantly that momentarily, like

children, we don't care if it never comes again.

1 EARLY

Sparklers

It almost hurts to look straight at it ...
my sister's outstretched burning sparkler,
that white-hot spider of light
where I must balance the unlit tip of my own
or it will never sputter to life,
and we'll never race down the evening beach,
whirling them at arms-length together.

Fog had slipped in off the Pacific.
After muffled rocket-pops from the pier,
the overhead murk would briefly blush
crimson, silver or blue.
But dashing into darkness,
we owned all the light we needed.
Heat-needles tingled hands.
Greasy smoke trailed us like scarves.

Yes, they would burn out soon
and we'd wander back up the beach,
find Mom tending our brother on a blanket
and Dad smoking Winstons in his folding chair.
Our parents loved us. They loved us equally,
perfectly. So we felt as children.

How fragile it all seems now.
How fragile it seems from this distance.
Sparklers reeling, electric against the night.
Twin strikes in the mind's eye
then extinguished, shrouded completely.
A family. A childhood.

House

We were all of us there. We three children
for the first time. Our house-proud father,
the brass door-key chain-trailing from his hand.

Our mother's holding my younger brother's,
her mind's-eye wandering room to room,
locating a sofa here, unrolling carpets there,

arranging tables and chairs to last the year
or a lifetime as it happened. Five lifetimes.
For there were five of us. Yes, and no one but us

exploring the coved-ceiling strangeness,
the heaviness of plaster-walled rooms, the elegant
rectangles of wan window-light crossing floors.

*

We kids opened cupboards, drawers. All empty,
as the ghostly thrumming refrigerator was empty.
As if no one had lived in this house before,

cooked here or slept, showered here or wept.
Though my sister, doing her best Nancy Drew,
insisted we search for a sign. Surely someone

left one or two tell-tales behind. We pulled off
shoes, half running, half skating in socks
across chestnut-colored floors and down

the t-shaped hall to rooms that drew us like heroes,
as if it was honor to first touch each closet's
end-wall, to slide gamely over cool yellow-tiled

bathroom floor. Nothing. We found nothing.
No washcloth in the tub. No residues of soap
at the sinks. No sign of any life but ours

until Mom called us to the back bedroom,
to a small framed photo barely noticeable
against roses of a faded, papered wall.

Dad lifted it from a nail, brought the frame
low and we five gathered to consider
the white-haired, dark-suited man

held at the waist by a wrinkled smiling woman,
his arm over the shoulder of a younger man
uniformed for war. They squinted

against bright California sun. They stood
beneath a stucco arch on the front porch
of this very house, now our house.

*

No way to ask what happened to the photo
as it's impossible now for Dad to recall
the rest of that day or those following

when movers trucked us across town, old house
to new. So much is lost as it happens forever.
Two months after he died I pulled Dad's suits

from his closet, removed each wood hanger,
folded coats and trousers, laid all but one in cartons,
drove the boxes to Goodwill. How the suits

smelled of him. And four years later I knelt
in the hall outside a bedroom where Mom
lay dying. I was sorting the sixty-year

clutter of family photos nestled in a drawer.
It wouldn't be long before I would take
what I wanted, before I'd walk the bare floors

with furniture sold off, packed off, gone.
For old time's sake I might take off my shoes.
But which photos would I choose?

And of what holiday? From which decade?
So many family faces topping navy blazers
and Easter dresses, floating above white-clothed

Thanksgiving tables. Before the house-sale closes
should I prop one frame on the mantle, one picture
to signify the lives that rose and fell inside?

But what new owner would care, or care enough.
And afterwards won't shadows still follow me
room to room, the years refuse to let go my hand.

The Polishings

In the warm painted porch of our old stucco house,
at the legged enamel laundry sink
covered with a plywood board,
my father taught me as he'd been taught,
how a salesman should polish his good shoes.

Make them shine enough to speak, he insisted.
They're your first step through the door.
He'd spread out newspaper, rags and brushes
and metal tins that twisted open with a pop,
revealing creams — deep brown, black, cordovan.

He taught me by doing with his own two hands:
a rag doubled to keep the gob of polish
from bleeding through; the non-master hand
like a foot inside the worked-on shoe
to hold it steady; the thorough
coating and spreading over leather

of waxy color, starting from scuffed toe
then down the instep-side to heel and back to toe.
Once both shoes were creamed over,
he lit a cigarette to let the glazed pair dry.
Hurried brushing, he'd say,
made a short-lived shine that wouldn't last half a day

of cold calls on the road. My father knew
so much in his handsome hands —
gilded with a rectangled wristwatch,
a wedding band, and between knuckles,
wiry sprays of golden hair. I can still see
one hand hidden inside a brogue, the other gripping

the wooden brush as it bristled out a leathered glow.
How long did they last
those lessons on the porch? One year? Two?
How long the morning polishings with the jobless day
before him, a son watching, a wife waiting
and no door but ours to walk through.

Mrs. Miller

And to the south lived dear old Mrs. Miller,
the first next door neighbor I really knew.
A doctor's widow. White-streaked, yellow hair.
With a nervous New York way of talking
though she'd lived out West for twenty years.

A grown daughter — Dorothy — lived with her,
worked somewhere, drove a red sports car.
Fruit trees grew behind their gabled house
and a crunching path of white crushed stone
ended at a Japanese-style fishpond.

I was tall enough then to climb the bamboo fence
and pull oranges from the tree that overhung
their pond. What fruit I couldn't reach, fell.
In January, you'd see lazy, blurred goldfish
tailing beneath navels floating on the pond.

Saturdays, I washed Mrs. Miller's Buick
with a bucket, soap and sponge. The fifteen cents
she paid was good money in '61. Later, on the lanai,
she'd pour my coke, wave away her cigarette smoke,
and engage me in grown-up conversation.

Since nothing ever goes according to plan, she'd say,
You'd think we'd figure out the plan.
I was at most eleven. She was a drunk, I suppose.
Confused, but open-hearted. Lonely, of course.
The first person like me I'd known.

His Hands

at our beginnings weren't impatient
or unloving, never careless or loosed

by drink. They held us as small children,
changed us, tickled us, tossed us, took good care

of us for after all we belonged to him.
And though youthful wills ran quick and strong,

our ideas remained small as our bodies,
failed to challenge him. Only once —

by then I was eleven — he whipped me
with a switch when I couldn't stop crying.

Forgotten now is whatever upset me.
Mom tried distraction, consolation,

but Dad stepped in, at a loss himself,
unable to bear his son's helpless crying.

For your own good, he insisted, marching me
out the back door. I remember the switch

of pale, slender wood though the strokes
didn't sting much ... not like the shock of it

happening at all, or the charge felt
facing him in the garage-gloom afterwards.

By nature he wasn't a hard man. But not
supple like that switch. And as our ideas

of our selves — my sister's, brother's and mine —
grew larger and larger, stronger and stranger,

Dad's hands gripped harder, heavied, yet felt
empty, as if we'd slipped his grasp.

Hunter

Out from under the pond-dam's narrow bridge
the otter slips down a sloped, stone sluice
and leaps the stream. Before vanishing,
she slides into a water-washed mound of branches,
a fish in her mouth, glittering silver as she runs.

Otter's long and brown-coated with a cat-like head
and hard useful tail. Reappearing empty-mouthed,
she trips up under the bridge again and I notice myself
thinking it's a she, a mother feeding her young.

Crossing the wood planks, I lean over to watch
down the dam's lake side. Otter enters
gray-green waters soundlessly, sleek and eel-like,
a foot beneath the pond's surface. Out she swims
and back. Hunting into the pond and back.

It's a gray morning at the worn bridge-rail.
I let everything go on. I'm hunting the world
for myself, can't yet grasp what I've found.
Somewhere in the pond's weedy deep a young pike

or bluegill hungers. Otter counts on that hunger.
She hunts from her needs as I do from mine. Soon
some fish will rise to feed, basking in shallows
the way thoughts do in the mind. As mine do now.
Otter leads to fish. Fish leads to trout and that ranger

promising the mountain lake well-stocked,
though Dad and I fished a long, hot afternoon
and caught nothing. We were already unhappy together
without knowing it, decades from knowing why.

At the bridge I'd wondered about the other otter,
the father otter. Was he elsewhere, not hunting?
I recognize now that my father tried his best
in 1962 when he quit his sales job for a better one
that didn't yet exist, never would exist.

Not his fault, that 60's recession. Months turned
to years and walking home from school I'd find him
shirt-sleeved in the yard or garage or kitchen
instead of Mom, off at her new secretarial job.

Not that she minded much or expected more.
She'd grown up poor. And when I call Dad a failure
I mean mostly in my mind of course, the place it hurts most.
Still, one day we stood on solid ground, stable.
The next a mid-air family, in pieces and falling.

As a boy I couldn't understand why he didn't do it right.
Or at least better. In my own life I tried. A man.
A father. Dad set the bar. A low bar you might suppose.
But it's not the bar itself. It's the need to be good enough.
To feed the hunger. To hunt for love and be fed.

Days later at the bridge I saw both otters hunting.
And decades after those sunburned hours of baiting hooks,
waiting in vain for a strike, Mom let slip
that Dad always hated fishing. Sometimes it's more
than I can bear, what my father bore for me.

It Rings

It rings in the night
and by day, through the rusting leaves
of our avocado tree. It rings
in the wire fence where
the neighbor's dog caught a paw
and bit my mother's arm
as she freed him.

There in the old yard
through an orange hoop
I shot baskets after school.
Strolling to the garage,
my father called for the ball.
He shot with two hands.
The hoop rings.

Always a white phone
in our kitchen. A black one
in the hall. They never rang
as mine rings now.
Awake or asleep doesn't matter.
It rings in the night.
It rings until you answer.

Taking Down the Tree

Those who decorate must undecorate,
our mother would declare come January
when the Christmas tree began shedding
dried-out needles everywhere to the floor.
So we reached down the bright glass balls,
the topping star, the odd, one-of-a-kind
ornaments. We wrapped them in newspaper,
nested them gently in a cardboard box.
And while Dad circled the tree, unwinding
the light-string, one of us coiled it up
at the plug-end, careful not to break
even one red, pointed bulb. We were doing
the clearing work that often follows joy,
itself a kind of second-hand joy. As for
the tinsel, my sister and I would've cast it
out to the street with our dead tree
but Mom voted us down. We saved
all we could, lifting off the foiled, dangling,
straw-like strands hung weeks before.
Some tangled inextricably. Others broke
when plucked from dry branches. The rest
we draped over a wrapping-paper tube
until they massed like a woman's hair,
light-trimmed, shimmering.

Dam

You could walk across that fifty-yard span,
paved like sidewalk on top. And we often did

on family walks in that high, arid valley.
We'd set out vacation-evenings after dinner

along a rough gravel road, passing
other brown cabins, ragged pines and scrub oaks,

uphill to the small, man-made California lake
and its concrete dam poured in the 1930s.

*

On the dam's lake side, pausing in a walk-across,
I could boost up on a railing of galvanized pipe

and look down on three or four fishermen
in painted wood boats casting green-black waters.

I sometimes balanced there, sensing the lake's
pressures, its immense, dam-checked, liquid weight.

On the walk's other side, as afterthought, a height
of chain-link fence had been welded to rail at midspan,

preventing bending over or staring down the dam's
sun-facing, nearly vertical wall. Only an outlying foot

of foundation was visible, and a white-bouldered
stream-bed vanishing into scrub a hundred feet below.

*

From that fence, over miles of descending valleys,
the eye naturally lifted up. In dusky minutes before stars,

with daylight green and gold over far mountains, the sky's
earth-returning color cast an ethereal, difficult blue.

And if the eye rode too far out into that sky
the mind was made to follow, as if an idea had formed

out there, a momentous idea that anyone on the dam,
everyone crossing it, must eventually endure.

*

So much I remember of our evening walks. My tall parents.
My self-conscious older sister. My impulsive

younger brother. I thought myself an ordinary boy. I longed
to be ordinary, playing baseball, watching sports on TV,

aligning myself as best I could with every convention. Yet
against that grain I sensed another purpose, and on our walks

I rehearsed a more perilous role, setting off alone
as we neared the dam's crossing, a brave scout and pathfinder.

*

One foot then another at the center of that scuffed
elevated lane. To my right the lake rose darkly, an enormous

presence testing the dam. On my left a nothingness of sky
that both drew and disturbed me. My sneakers scraped

the gritty walk. And sometimes I stopped at mid-crossing,
calling back to my family a few simple words,

some poetry, to assure the others of safe passage
through a world I couldn't yet know. *All clear,* I cried,

as if a boy's intention could guide or protect, as if love
might shelter the distances we had together to go.

2 LATER

Polk Street

I don't remember who chose the shabby tavern
on Polk Street three blocks north of Market,
only that we landed there afternoons after another

tedious law school class, lounging at its lacquered
mahogany bar near the square, filthy, street-facing
plate-glass window and its neon MILLERS sign.

There was the one ancient bartender coughing
his smoker's cough in the shadows, and an erratic
overhead flickering from bare-bulb fluorescents,

and liquor stocks shelved before a mirror reflecting
both a second image of each bottle and our own
two faces stenciled by the bar's tinseled, mirrored light.

No doubt you know a place like it. There must be
a thousand places like it. But no other with my sister
on the high leather stool beside me, lighting up

a mentholed Newport, sipping her vodka martini,
still droll and sun-blonde, fresh and wicked-clever
and cocky at twenty-eight for all her weaknesses.

I'd complain about our dull professors. She would
make me laugh as only she could, turning the hour
privileged and superb, reducing our current troubles

to brief stations we'd glide through effortlessly
together. Carolyn would do good work in the years
ahead. She would draft laws still on the books

in California, and before drink took over her life
she made the world better for people. For many
people, those who know her work maintain.

They say you can't go back but I ask what matters
more after everything that happens. My sister slips
a Newport from its box. I strike a match and watch

the red glow of tobacco igniting as her cigarette
nears my half-cupped hand. Fruitless maybe,
but I go back anyway, if only to save

the merest fraction of her liveliness,
even just the match-light flaring her face.
Though doubtless she'd argue, if she could,

that I also return for last word in our life-long debate.
Calling for a fresh martini, swinging on her stool
back my way, Carolyn cheerfully tries

to persuade me again — and seriously,
as if to persuade us all — that nothing,
neither she nor I nor anything else, can be saved.

Spent

As for dying, she often said she didn't mind
so very much except for the expense.

My mother talking about money
was my mother talking about life.

The sticky grips on dad's wheelchair.
Odorous nights when she'd catch the sob

from his rented bed, knowing
he'd soiled the sheets again. No.

By expense she meant not the money drain
but how time went and went

until even the clocks felt empty.
Serious in her faith she'd question me late

about prayers unanswered . . . what it meant
when even her loving God felt spent.

Crying Man

At O'Hare, after a first jump west to California,
I thought my father was dying, as I waited

for the connecting flight. Being hungry
I ate pizza with the people eating pizza.

Feeling uninformed, I bought a newspaper,
opened magazines at the bookshop wall.

Near my gate, I pretended not to watch
a dozen others waiting, as they pretended

not to watch me. But finally, in a hectic airport
restroom, I heard the crying man in his stall.

Oh God, he cried, behind a stained steel door.
He didn't sound old. And in his privacy, not shy.

Oh Dear God, rang harshly in the close tiled room.
I stood alongside others, a simple traveler

at a public urinal. Behind me the restless waited
their turns. *Oh dear life* came the third cry.

I shook myself, zipped, found a vacant sink
for washing. Spurting water dwindled on my hands.

I lathered and rinsed as I'd been taught. Grabbed
for paper towel. At the mirror, did not linger.

Turtle

Out of the pond across the tar road and uphill
to my yard probably took half a day,
though when I found him dug in behind the shed
among last fall's leaves, when at the third tap of my rake
a hooked head and yellow eyes
emerged from his broad, scarred shell,
I chose to believe he'd simply lost his way.

Wasn't it a kindness to slide a snow shovel
under him? And wasn't I fulfilled
by the downhill drag of his weight,
by the slight splash as I tipped him into the shallows,
watched gray-green, half-armored legs stretch out
and nailed feet paddle weakly away.

Not unlike the way my father's hands had waved
weakly as the orderly wheeled his gurney
down the rehab-wing hall. Not seeing me,
Dad plucked ineffectually at his IV line. Later,
waking to me standing at the foot of his bed,
he begged as if I were the parent to take him home.

We tell ourselves ordinary life will return
after death, after grief. But it's only
the extraordinary departing. Meanwhile,
more work for the nurses.
Spittle gathers on an old man's chin.
A driven turtle labors up the hill again.

It was August, steaming hot. A wild stink
surrounded the shed. Extruded now from their shell
legs and head swelled grotesquely.
At first I stepped back. Who doesn't at first step back.

But drawn closer I saw the insect multitude,
the host of ruby-tinged bodies swarming the flesh.
Call it natural. Call it mortal. In its way even beautiful.
Yet later that week wasn't I also grateful
that some sleek and secret animal
stole into my yard by night, bore the body away.

Light of the World

Bedbound and finally helpless to stand, he couldn't
piss without a plastic tube or hurt anyone but himself
anymore. And because I was flying home that morning

I leaned beside his bed, said, *I may not see you again.*
Dad paused for breath. Like a child and with a child's
sweetness he whispered, *You'll never stop me loving you.*

There was a decade we didn't speak. He didn't once visit
my kids. He thought it mattered when he changed his will,
when he later changed it back. Meanwhile I wrote him letters.

Every day another black letter. All in my mind of course.
And now? Soon he would be dead. Yet even bent to his deaf ear
the truth struggled in my throat. *Goodbye Dad,* I said.

Alone in a cab down the long airport road I listened
to words I couldn't say. And in years since,
on rush hour trains, in grocery store lines, in courtrooms

and bathrooms, on winter beaches alone. Even
on brightest days here with a clear-eyed sun blazing
light-of-the-world forgiveness, even when I fathom

the nature within the nature of love ... still, the truth can't
change. I used to shock friends, saying I hated my father.
I meant, I couldn't yet forgive myself for loving him.

How to Fold a Wheelchair

Lock one wheel.
Face the chair.
At midline pinch
and lift the flesh-
colored
plastic seat.

As it folds upward
the two padded
arm-rests and
wheeled sides can't
help but pull
together

until where a man
once sat
they almost
touch.

November Wind

Now having years outlived my father who am I
to complain of plane trees peeling in the parkways,
or a brick-building view of cloud-smoked sky,
or yet another rainless autumn week, the guttered
leaves all rust and brown and speechless at my feet
as if laid down for some November wind to blow
where it will as St. John says the spirit blows.

*

That frigid winter day with my father at the beach
a sudden offshore wind swirled up storms of sand.
Stinging grains flew everywhere. Painful to a boy
anyway. I could barely open my eyes. But grabbing
my arm, he said, *Get behind me.* And I did. Such things
happen. In the lee of him I gripped his jacketed back,
leaned against his bones, opened my eyes to curtains
of seething sand gusting the wave-plowed shore.

*

No doubt his lids closed until the storm passed.
Now his storm has passed. His mouth sewn shut.
His eyes. While here on this fleeting street
my own wind arrives from every direction.
And the leaves cry out, *Open your eyes!*
But where is my shield? Even his weakness
would serve me now. Even his failures
guide me. O where is the shadow he cast for me?

Remembering Herself Remembering

No blood or broken bone, thank heavens,
    only her forehead glancing off the counter
going down and an almost pleasant fuzziness
    to the windowed sunlight afterwards
as she looked up from the tiled kitchen floor.
    Had the little dog tangled her underfoot,
she wondered. She didn't worry for herself
    but standing, she dialed the doctor because
she couldn't remember, she couldn't quite
    remember where her husband might be
and who if not her was caring for him.
    Her hands tingled. The receiver pulled heavy
as stone. Yet she steadied, firmed on her feet
    as the nurse, the doctor's kind nurse,
answered questions and reminded her.
    Well she laughed then, unexpectedly,
and companionably the nurse laughed too.
    A freedom to laugh together. At lunch
she laughed again with her son, remembering
    herself that morning remembering.
Imagine, she said. *Even death you forget.*

3 THEN

Carolyn

Not yet of two minds that raw hospital afternoon
when the decade-long charade of my sister's diabetes

as explanation for everything difficult and strange
happening to her broke down, and the on-call doctor

declared what I'd suspected long before entering
Carolyn's house that morning and finding in a cupboard

twenty or more empty quart bottles of Jim Beam
bourbon. *Your sister's an alcoholic,* the doctor

told me in the hall, then said it to both of us
once we entered her room, putting on

a grave and certain manner, remarking that liquor
was suicide for an insulin-dependent diabetic.

No surprise when Carolyn disagreed.
Propped in bed in a lank hospital gown, her dyed

and bowl-cut brown hair in greasy disarray,
my sister stiffened, insisted otherwise, her manner

briefly charged with authority, as if channeling
the keen-witted lawyer she'd once been.

*

The doctor said she'd happily review the literature
but declined discharge until my sister agreed in writing

to a treatment plan. Carolyn turned on me then.
Why had I flown out to Oakland, interfering as always.

From a shopping bag I'd filled at her house, I stood upright
on the foot of her bed six empty bourbon bottles, the big

red B centered on each label, the brand-name in fancy
script above the words *Not Genuine Without the Signature.*

As from a great distance Carolyn regarded the bottles.
Fondly she looked, with a childlike pleasure and intimacy,

and argued no further when I supported the doctor,
said I wouldn't let her die this way, meaning I had another

in mind, a longer way which I imagined better, though
my sister had already decided, no nursing home

for her, no selling her house to pay for care. No. No. No.
None of that for her. She was smart and stubborn

like other women in our family. Farmers' wives, teachers,
nurses who often outlived their Arkansas, Montana

or Iowa husbands for decades in righteous judgment,
in futile longings and suppressed Presbyterian fury.

*

I took Carolyn home. I remained for a time, driving her
to AA meetings which she attended willingly so long

as I stayed in Oakland, kept her company. Riding home
from meetings she'd describe those who'd spoken that day.

A few interesting or inspiring. Many neither. Yet all comical
in her accounts during those two weeks before I flew home.

I couldn't stay. I had my own life. I didn't want to stay.
Carolyn exhausted me, even in her sobriety. Especially

in her sobriety. Which continued afterward with phone calls
at night and stories from meetings, though the AA tales

dwindled before long. Her night calls rang later and later,
her telephone voice loosened, as did her thinking

and humor. She waxed nostalgic and sentimental, recalling
our childhoods, her first marriage, her second. Soon

I realized she was keeping company with Jim Beam again,
her true and faithful brother, her protector against

what she called the unendurables, arriving like clockwork
each afternoon except when they appeared at breakfast.

*

Nine months later she fell off her back porch one night,
landed face down in a garden path. Which was the end

of that part of Carolyn, who I loved, who I couldn't stop
loving in the way I couldn't help trying, misguidedly,

to save her. For what does saving a person mean?
I think of those bottles upright on my sister's hospital bed,

her fond regard for their labels, the stale remainders
of air, the brown bourbon-crusts circling bottoms.

As If For A Journey

she's dressed in plain, clean clothes
and sensible shoes. Someone combed
her chopped-off, brown-dyed hair,
applied a trace of pink to gloss lips
and powder to color her gray, fine-lined,
smoker's cheeks. No cheap bourbon
smell on her breath. No whiff of cigarettes.
Only a slight, oddly comforting, chemical
smell — as of cleanser or preservative —
which somehow suggests eternity,
about which my brilliant alcoholic sister
speculated endlessly, her curiosity
knocking on inner windows of disbelief.
She was three when I was born, sixty
years ago. I won't see her face again.
Her spirit's gone, as she'd wish it gone,
to that place of knowledge where a last
bearable secret is revealed. If there is
such a place or secret. If beyond the body
even one revelation waits to be known.

Oakland

Thursday was trash day but I'd forgotten until
a garbage truck groaned through my sister's
ramshackle neighborhood, jerked me awake
at dawn with another electric thought
of failure ... I'd tired early the day before,
neglected to drag the half-dozen
trash-stuffed, plastic bags out to the street.

From an upstairs window I watched the truck
hulk past, trailing its stink of calamity
and waste. Too late now to call, *Wait! Come back!*
Too late to forget Carolyn's way
of cocking her head, eyes-rolled at some folly
of her own, or mine. Stupid grief. Everything
forgotten but what you want to forget.

She'd have mocked me, and my distress
over those plump, porch-stranded black bags.
No call for her things now. Not the greasy,
dime-store slippers or years of unopened
bank statements. Not the stack of bourbon-stained
gardening magazines or the icy
beef-packets and murky insulin vials
my knife pried loose from a frost-choked fridge.

Not rid of me yet, boyo! She'd have crowed
if beside me at the window now,
tickled that the house clean-out and sale had fallen
to me, delighting in my failure

to finish it. *Not rid of her yet!*
But how I then longed to be, watching
the trash truck distancing, its groan now
a fading moan down the dawning street.

O sister! My maddening, self-harming
sister! Yet the same one who ten summers
before drew me to a downstairs window
overlooking her garden, to consider
the flowering, cultivated beds. Taking
my arm, she named natives — Prickly Phlox,
Fleabane Daisy, California Poppy —
schooled me to notice how each bloom played
originally within its greens.

Childless, with only the black Lab Lucy
for company in her stick Victorian,
Carrie was mid-way through her last act,
working part-time, half-managing the drinking.
That afternoon we walked her pleasant yard,
past honeysuckle hedges and along
the very palm-shaded path where a neighbor
found her. How casually
we talked. Always there would be more to say.

Reward

Call them our reward, those long, free California
mornings the last few years after the second death
and how openly we'd speak in bathrobes
at the breakfast table, me sipping a decaf,
Mom with her ginger tea. One of us saying,
Remember when ... and the other responding,
Wasn't that the night the Ford broke down?
Or one pressing the other, *What was the guy's*
name who ... And we'd laugh and laugh over
what had happened, meaning our past, meaning
in retrospect, meaning how ridiculous
and misguided our worries and angers
had usually been, not then knowing how life
turns out, neither right nor wrong in the end.
No tears those mornings. Only laughter.
Even recalling Dad's furies after
his parking-lot crash, when cops took away
his license and the DMV failed him
in test after desperate driving test. *He became*
a different person, Mom offered. *Yes and*
no, I reminded her, having by then
talked out together this great family
mystery — loving husband for sixty
years who also played bad father to three
children — and the denial Mom kept up
until those bitter, no-driving years
when his cruelty turned, falling at last on
her. But only after Dad was gone
did she change sides and finally put to rest

her wifely duty to defend. Some say
that truth like freedom only passes heart
to heart. If so, by now ours had traveled us,
delivered us, granted us those few
survivor-bright, breakfast-table mornings.
Remember, we would say. *Just remember.*
And our hard times returned less hard,
the sweet, sweeter still in remembrance.

In the Ferny Bracken

1.

In that recliner chair at night, her swollen feet up,
alone after Dad died, she'd listen to jazz
on the radio and read her novels,
much as on long-ago afternoons home from work
she read to relax on a backyard chaise-longue,
her upper body and book shaded by our avocado tree,
bare legs and sandled feet extended into the sun.

2.

It was after the second stroke, during rehab at UCLA,
when Mom asked me to read aloud
a romance novel my younger brother Dave
brought to the hospital from her house.
It was one of a stack of thick, big-print versions
she'd regularly check out from the public library
and read evenings at home in the black chair
where Marcia the housecleaner found her one morning
unable to rise, lacking power of speech.

3.

The nurses whispered my great luck
in having such a mother. At ninety-six she amazed
the staff with her wry humor and determination,
though when I first arrived from the airport
Mom's speech garbled, a crimped left hand

lay useless in her lap. Yet she came back.
In time it all came back. Therapists worked her
each morning, one demanding routine after another.

4.

On the sixth day, under a thin blanket, her gray head
tipped my way, Mom lay abed as I read,
her blue eyes half-closed, glasses reflecting sunlight
from tall, hospital-room windows.
The novel contained the usual English manor house
overlooking a rocky shore, the usual beautiful
wealthy young widow visiting friends for a weekend,
and the usual brooding, handsome ship captain
returned home from an 18th-century war.

5.

Though it seemed far longer, the novel's account
of their lovemaking in the ferny bracken
lasted but two pages. But reading into it,
I noticed the room growing warm.
I must've paused, for Mom asked, sympathetically,
Sweetie, is reading this making you uncomfortable?
Oh, no, no, I answered. *Not at all.*
We laughed. I read on. And on.
Pretty graphic stuff, I said, the lovers spent at last.
But not that unrealistic, Mom replied.
Well, lucky you, I said. And she smiled a secretive smile.

6.

I'd sat with Mom at breakfasts after Dad died,
and now in that bright hospital room
we kept company again, reading on
as widow and captain made their way back
to the manor house in awkward, post-coital joy.
There would be warm afternoons when Mom
seemed to be dozing off and I'd pause my reading.
No, no. Go on. I'm still here, she'd murmur,
waving her hand. Evenings I'd drive back
to our old house, trying for sleep in a bedroom
once shared with my brother,
or walking the familiar, dark-furnitured rooms
before settling in Mom's black recliner-chair.

7.

Those nights I fell into — what to call it? —
this new reality, a preview of grief before
the real grief. I'd worry details of her return home.
I'd wonder how much time we had, how her end
would come. Eventually drifting off in the big
chair, I'd dream. Several nights the same dream
with me blanketed in that hospital-room bed
while Mom sat on a hard chair, reading aloud.
Her book told the story of our family
good times, yes, but not leaving out the troubles
and when Mom finished a chapter

we'd talk quietly, intimately.
More than once I said to her, *I'll miss you,*
and she'd reply, laughingly,
You'll only miss me because I know how to read.

8.

Once on a break from reading I told Mom
my dream. Window blinds glowed with late-day
sun, and listening down the length of her bed,
she took off her glasses, her face composed,
calm as when we kids used to pester her,
trying to make her admit which of us she loved best.
Remember me telling you once, she said,
that your father was the most important person to me?
I remembered a phone call, early in the years
after I moved East, cut myself off from the family.
You never needed me that way, she continued.
You only thought you did. But how I hated saying it.
Ruefully, I said, *You knew me too well.*
And for your whole life, she agreed.

9.

There was an evening when Mom seemed
too restless for reading. When she said she wanted
to say goodbye, I stood up, thinking
she'd tired, needed to be alone.
But she shook her head, gestured me to sit.

I meant, she said, *I want us to say*
our goodbyes now while I have my wits back
and you're here with me.
OK, I said. But doubtfully.
A counsellor recommended it, she explained.
OK, I said again, reaching out,
and she laid her gray-veined hand in mine.
We sat in the quiet evening hospital,
waiting for the other to speak.
After a few minutes, Mom sighed.
I guess we're not ready yet, she said.

10.

But we held hands longer, the way
you do sometimes with a dear person,
not waiting on the future or expecting
return, not marking time or accomplishment,
just holding and being held until
the hand forgets to whom it belongs.
Was it only our years together
that seemed to sift down and settle
like a blessing, like lamplight?
Yet I remember the effort
love demanded even then. As always,
sorrow was ours to resist or admit.
Soon each must let go the other's hand.

Ready

When foiled by her worsening memory,
when a void rose where familiar names
should be, Mom would exclaim on the phone,
Oh you know who I mean! And when I didn't
she'd declare, *Well it will come to me.*
And the next day or evening she'd ring back
to report that the young man she'd remembered
when we last talked, the one who played
tenor saxophone in her high school band,
was Frank McGrath . . . and the not-too-bright
blonde he dated was Elizabeth, though
everyone called her Betty. These recallings
and reportings I took to be another exercise,
like her mornings on the stationary bike
when pedaling hard she'd recite in order
the mostly Spanish names of her town's
cross-streets — *Georgina, Carlyle, Margarita,*
Alta — as far south as her memory would go.

She was ninety-eight, turning ninety-nine,
but never called about street names . . . only
about the people, her people. She didn't want
me to wonder, be mistaken, or suppose they
didn't matter. *We all have a name,* she'd say.
And everyone has a people. She'd cared
for hers but often now felt them departing,
Passing down a darkening street, as she put it.
Hence her need to remember their names,
that she might call out to the right ones.

If that's allowed, she'd add, trusting
her beloveds would turn on the street,
would wave to her and wait. Without
saying so, she was telling me she'd prepared
and was ready to join her people.

Six months later, her readiness made it
easier to follow physician orders
and withhold food and water. Easier
at least until she woke fearfully,
angrily one morning, saying in words
among her last to me that we'd made
a terrible mistake and I must call Dr. Wolfe,
that she was unbearably thirsty and everything
was so wrong. It was as if she'd found herself
on a street of strangers, and the names
so carefully remembered ... each beloved
name useless, homeless, summoning no one.

With the Door Left Open Should Mom Cry Out

The rainstorm such a furious row
on the patio's plastic roof
that joining my chair-slumped, smoking brother
I must shout to bum a cigarette.

Dave shakes one loose
and at his lighter's click, a candle-like flame
makes of us a ceremony, a communion
close as any we've known.

Our downpour pounds on grievously.
Between us the glow and pall
of burning cigarettes. Again, death closes.
Soon, impossibly, only we two will be left.

A Few Minutes After Nine

1.

He woke naturally to the slow, much-alike
mornings. Bed-rails chroming brighter at dawn.
Room-lamps paling. Windows sluggishly filling
with light. Now his fourth week of manning
the five-to-noon shift since arriving
from the East Coast. Now the old house again
imperceptibly coming to life
as he fulfilled promises made to her
and to himself: he would stay to the end;
he would feel whatever there was to feel;
he would remember how death came for her.

2.

So he had prepared, opening himself
morning after morning to the possible hour,
to the appearance and recognition
whenever it came. It came without warning
that Tuesday. First felt as a quickening,
then as an exquisite intimacy,
a solemn concentration entering
her bedroom. He felt joined by it. Joined to it.
Pictures on walls loomed closer. Her vasolined
lips parted as if to speak, though she was now
days beyond speech. Her brow smoothed. Her breath
dwindled, lulled. Or what he thought was a lull.
Then it happened. A few minutes after nine.

No other breath. Only a final flutter
as flesh sank at the folds of her neck,
his mother's delicate parting move.

3.

He wasn't disappointed. This wasn't
an occasion for disappointment. Yet
he'd hoped for more. Selfishly, he'd wanted
a last sign or gesture. Or more grandly,
more beautifully, he'd hoped to witness
as in a dream or poem, bright soul released
from worn body. Was it so wrong, his longing
at the last for her imperishable self,
the spirit he'd known his whole life by way
of feeling? Why not show herself plainly
in a last dance before vanishing?
But as it happened he sensed no presence,
no release or escape, no confirmation
of his mother's faith. Nothing to console
beyond a dry sense of accomplishment,
that the last task they'd ever conceive
and carry out together was achieved.

4.

Her mouth had fallen open. Standing over her,
he saw a gray, fissured tongue, yellowed teeth.
His hands reached to close the mouth, held it closed ...

as days before a nurse had suggested,
whispering, *Before rigor sets in.*
Her chin felt warm. And either from that touch
or his letting go, a greater feeling rose.
Not mourning or sorrow. Not spiking grief.
But a child-like sense of discovery,
an excitement, as if truth's long-hidden shape
had been thrillingly revealed. It was so simple.
She had loved him. He'd loved her. So obvious.
Yet suddenly amazing. She was gone.
He remained. Also amazing. He longed
to speak, to summon right and perfect words
for unexpected joy. Why be sorry?
She'd lived her life. Now was dead. Forever
and always dead. She was complete and he was glad.

5.

Soundlessly a digit on her bedside clock
changed. He caught sight of the movement, noted
the time, as a nurse had also instructed.
From an open jar of skin cream on the bureau
a familiar fragrance. And gradually
in the spare morning light his exaltation
drained. What to do now? Whom must he call?
But he remained in his chair, registering
bed-blanket drape, the body's absolute
stillness. He grew aware of an unfamiliar
silence — the stitch, stitch, unspooling thread

of a particular silence — then rising
in him, mixing with the quiet moment,
a memory of the ancient camellia bush
outside her bedroom window where now —
just as some fifty years before when
she'd call him to witness the eerie hoverings —
a hummingbird fed on scarlet flowers.

4 AFTER

Afterwards

1.

As if a switch in me or many switches
had been thrown. As if the presence of two
black-suited men rolling the sheet-draped body
from bedroom to hall and out our mother's
front door had somehow cast the world into
higher definition, with each sound and bar
of light suddenly cutting-sharp, and our senses
flourished by chrome-flashing gurney rails
and rubber-wheeled squelches on wood floors,
by the faint scent of the mortician's sheet
and the conclusive, closing thunk of a van door.

2.

Through too-brilliant California morning streets,
driving to breakfast with my brother Dave and
his wife Sue, distortions continued. At the diner
a cook's smeared apron glowed with egg-yolk yellows
and tomato-sauce reds. A raucous kitchen
clattered with dishes being stacked. Our waitress'
gardenia-like perfume lingered long after
she'd jotted orders in her pad and slipped off
into the murmur-slurry of surrounding customer's
half-heard conversations. Their chatter melded
with the ongoing clink and scrape of cutlery
on plates, with moist sounds of people at their food,
while overhead fluorescents harshly lit innocent
and not so innocent faces. As for us, seated now
in a booth, all of it — every particle, tone and tick of it —
entered us like wind rushing through an open door.

3.

So much life afterwards. Too much life it seemed.
I saw strain in Sue's drawn expression, in Dave's
trembling hand, spooning sugar after sugar
into his coffee. My own distress was more disbelief,
kin to one from thirty years before, after my son's
thirty-six hour birth. For weeks following
pushing his carriage along Berkeley streets,
I was amazed by each hurrying student and
slow elder, each deliveryman on rounds.
Like my son, all had been born of a woman.
Each survived the risky adventure of birth.
Amazed was my word that year. I was amazed
by life ... how it begins in helplessness
and danger then powers up with seemingly
unlimited needs and energy. Unstoppable
and everlastingly forceful each human life
seemed to me in those long-ago days.

4.

But in the diner now, an opposite astonishment.
Now our frailty struck me: the flaw
designed into our imperfect machines; the inevitable
dooms and vanishings never to be undone.
I seemed to see absences everywhere present,
like shrouds or shadows suspended over
the customers, trailing every waitress and cook.
While across the table from me Dave and Sue
and their usual cheerful intensities were now
shaded by similar foreshortenings. They looked

so temporary, as if, were I momentarily
to lower my eyes, they might well be taken,
gone before I could glance up again.

5.

We spoke fitfully, quietly. We sipped coffees.
Our waitress slid plates of richly-smelling
food before us and my brother raised his fork,
tentatively tasted his eggs, began eating.
Sue did the same. Room-noise seemed to lower
as if one in charge had turned the volume down,
and I noticed two, small, pleasant paper cups
served with my tostada, one of guacamole,
the other of sour cream. Then I too was tasting,
chewing, swallowing. And only much later,
well after we'd finished eating and the waitress
freshened our coffees, did I glance about
the diner, now ordinary in all respects,
see Dave and Sue again solidly themselves.

6.

Only for a moment, recalling our mother's
shape on the gurney, did I feel half-undone, as if
I'd failed to honor her suffering, or hold fast
to the vision I'd been granted. Yet how sensibly
I defended myself, reframing my morning insight
as a normal play on exhaustion and grief.
Better to release and look less far ahead,

to gather and move on. For wasn't our day
just beginning, with tasks to accomplish,
arrangements to be made? We paid the bill,
stepped into Southern California sunshine.
And as traffic flew by on Wilshire Boulevard,
I was already feeling again — preposterous
as this sounds, foolish as it seemed to me even
then — that with others walking that sidewalk
Dave and Sue and I would live forever.

Olympic Valley

On holiday I woke early, stepped out to see
morning come to the mountains. The valley's

quiet before dawn was the idea of night
I love best. Somewhere birds were thinking

of singing. And from the cabin's deck I felt
everywhere drawn up through a blue-black,

star-backed crown of trees. All week had been
a year since the third funeral. Now daybreak.

And it seemed only fair, only natural that
the weight of sad times should be lifting.

Along ridged mountain-dark stretched a lining
of chemical fire. And as morning heavened

east to west, a watercolor wash of blues and
corals bled skyward. Don't ask for too much,

I told myself. Fair has nothing to do with it.
Yet I held to that sky later, to the chill night

passing, how stars went out one by one by
one and a new sun rose over the valley.

Rain

I was caught pacing a back road beneath tunneling
October trees when the downpour began   a hard
windless New England rain from nowhere   in no time
storm-sounds desolate overhead   first heard
as a rustling   then as continuous crackling   eventually
almost a burning as drops by the thousands struck
innumerable thousands of leaves   any one of which
near-silent in isolation   yet taken together becoming
a power   a wild overhead racketing as I turned for home
oaks and maples early shielded but their canopy
soon released its own wet gatherings   here and there
smacking the road or my head or shoulder with drops
larger than any raindrop   at the wood's end a path
to my house wound uphill across steep unmowed
fields   I stopped under a last dripping tree   gray aqueous
light gloamed the field   it was a light reminiscent
while the rain-sound also rang familiar   mysteries
that drove me from shelter and into the storm   hurrying
up the track   almost jogging   hair soaked   thin
coat clinging to my back   both curious and not   both
trying to reach a lost point of memory and avoiding it

Thirty yards from home I stopped to look back   wires
of rain and a gray radiance clean as wet pearls over
the steep field   then remembering a light   this very
light falling from bedroom windows   and a downpour
almost tropical in suddenness two nights before
she died   such a hard rain so rare in Southern California
that hearing it rattle the patio roof at first I hadn't realized

it was rain   more a groaning   steady as a machine
and now the same light as when I kept company
that month in the family home   it had fallen on her bed
on bedclothes and body those last mornings I sat
beside her   and with the same conclusive silence
waiting   the same expectancy I now felt standing in
the field   my own house within sight   yellow lights
in windows   a soaked hillside below   rain hard
on me   dripping me   yet sure the storm would pass

I'd wanted sorrow to end before it began   I'd meant her
passing to leave me somehow less alone   and so I
willed myself not to miss her   as if that thread might be
pulled and trimmed from my close-woven life   rivulets
ran scalp to forehead   I wiped my eyes   it was only
water   it was only love and the persistent touch of rain
my missing my mother would go on as I'd go on   now
it tremored me warmly   finally fully running me through
noiselessly the rain fell   hissing as it struck ground   the wet
bent grasses telling another story of rain   loose soil turned
to mud underfoot   unabsorbed water coursed and pooled
as gravity demanded   down low-leaning skies and over
sloped fields it fell while her absence rose in me   a hill

Treasure

The payphone far-ending the night-dark truck stop
demands no coin of me, so again and
again I dial the number inked in blue
on a self-addressed envelope propped
on the booth's shelf. Under a small-bulb's
wan flicker, I misread the numbers,
dial wrongly over and over, while the booth's
folding door pinches inward, rattled
by fever-dry, Mojave winds. Finally
connecting, after a long ringing, I hear
my sister's voice ask, *Why are you calling me*
again in a dream? Years have gone by.
The story of how she chose to die leads
nowhere, never ends but in dial-tone resuming,
a receiver laid to rest, tears appearing
suddenly on the envelope, dissolving
her number to a washed-out, cerulean blue.
Doubtless a color to make sense of later.
Some endings I'll make sense of never. Hence
her voice, called up across enormous country.
It's treasure, what the nights put me through.

Cedars of Lebanon

Place me like a seal over your heart,
Like a seal on your arm.
For love is stronger than death,
its jealousy unyielding as the grave.

SONG OF SOLOMON

1.

For a long time I didn't much care for the trees,
those enormous parkway evergreens, one planted
before each house along our block. Already old
when I was young, squat and huge at the base,
with many straight thick branches that overhung
yards and parked cars, they shaded our house
during all seasons from afternoon sun. Early on
I discovered the trees made for poor climbing;
Gummy, invisible, half-dried sap clung to the bark,
invariably came off on my hands.
While even at a distance they made their presence felt,
all year long raining short sharp needles
that prickled and stung anyone walking barefoot
on our front lawn. For most of my life I thought
them native California pines and learned only recently
they're Cedars of Lebanon, transplants
from ancient Mediterranean forests, their name familiar
from bible readings, their wood prized by Pharaohs
for great temples, by Phoenicians for ships of trade.

2.

As a boy I prized the trees for nothing particularly
        and I'd still believe them pines but for my visit
to the neighborhood two years after Mom died.
        My brother and I sold the house to a developer
whose agent claimed he planned to live there
        with his family, a lie which would've appealed
to our parents who hoped their beloved house would
        pass on, be enjoyed by others. But we received
only one offer. Two years later, visiting my daughter
        in Los Angeles, I drove by the house because
it seemed a good son's duty — like kneeling at graveside,
        or laying flowers on a cemetery stone.

3.

But by then our house was no longer a house.
        I figured it would've disappeared. Months
after the sale I'd driven by, witnessed the tear-down
        begun behind a chain-link construction fence.
Weeds choked the gardens. Stripped from the roof,
        red clay tiles lay grounded in shards, piled near
a rusting dumpster. I didn't stop. Maybe I should have.
        Maybe a story was waiting for me there
in the front lawn gone to seed. Maybe a better one,
        I thought two years later after I'd parked
my rental car and stood on the sidewalk before a fancy
        two-story, nearly finished, beach-style, spec house.

High on his ladder a house-painter brushed
        shingles a glossy white. I watched him work.
He descended, walked the ladder along the house,
        climbed again with rags, bucket and brush.
Old house. Gone house. I'd hoped to be touched
        by anger or resentment, by regret, or even
gratitude, but felt only disappointment for a wasted trip.

4.

The street was quiet, with no cars passing,
        no dogs out for a walk or children playing.
Turning to my car, I noticed a yellow paper stapled
        to one parkway tree, a legal notice from the city
that this tree was scheduled to be cut down.
        Under the heading "Reason for Removal,"
I read the words "DYING TREE" and looking up
        saw bare limbs and a few remaining pockets
of brown needles. The notice read "Cedar of Lebanon"
        and immediately there rose boyhood memories
of sitting bored in church, hearing the ancient trees
        mentioned in Scripture readings. I stood close,
before and beneath the great tree. It smelled
        dry and pungent, and when I touched the bark
a more specific image rose: myself at eight or nine
        standing on tip-toes at our kitchen sink,
unable to wash the sticky pitch off my hands
        after climbing this very front-yard tree. Memory
played like a movie, full of color, detail

and sound. My mother stood at the stove cooking.
I could hear Carolyn reading to my younger brother
in the next room. The pitch wouldn't dissolve
with soap or scrub off with a sponge, and as warm
tap water beaded over gray, stubborn stains
on my hands, I complained bitterly. Mom stepped close,
recognized the problem, called to my father
who appeared in the doorway, tall as ever,
a cigarette burning in his freckled right hand.

5.

Unnerving to re-enter a scene, six decades gone.
On the street I was aware of standing in two places
at once. Before me rose the aromatic cedar.
Yet there also stood Mom and Dad, my brother
and sister, the old tiled kitchen in all its physicality
with everything and everyone lively as once
they'd been. I knew my father would know what to do
and he did, balancing his smoke on the counter-edge,
retrieving from a cupboard a yellow can of lighter fluid,
squirting liquid on a rag and rubbing my hands
until pitch dissolved and the skin cleared.
Tossing the rag into the trash, Dad retrieved
his cigarette and told me to wash now with soap
and hot water, adding wryly I should consider
wearing gloves the next time I climbed that tree.
Eagerly I washed at the sink, but though free
of pitch my hands now smelled of lighter fluid.
So I washed again, then again, each time smelling
my hands, each time certain the acrid smell remained.

6.

On tip-toes at the sink, I'm aware of also standing
before a parkway cedar, some sixty years later,
close to our now demolished house. I'd seen my parents
on their death beds. Yet here they both stood,
youthful, busy, fully themselves again.
And it was splendid to be with them,
with feelings too large to explain except to say
they were the free feelings of childhood,
that feeling of being with my family again.
Splendid, yes. But far from untroubled.
For an aura clung to the scene, a painful awareness
that I was both recalling our past
and living on after so much had happened.
The hurt rose from knowing these two places
and times could not long stay aligned.
Still, my hands smelled of lighter fluid.
Warm water fell from the tap. Mom had returned
to the stove while Dad smoked in the doorway.
Yet all the while, late in my own life, I stood beneath
clear Southern California skies,
shaded by a great, resinous, dying tree.
And gone from my mind was any plan
to make more of a scene which until now had been lost
and inconsequential to me. What I wanted,
all that I longed for, with desire only sharpened
by impossibility, was that my visit home,
this being again with the family, might last.

The Return

Years later, I entered their light on a Tuesday,
parked on a quiet, mostly empty, New Haven street.
Nothing much happened. No urgent cars rushed by.

No wind bothered the trees. Now and then a bird
flew low, wings flashing. Also, over dry lawns,
a few butterflies. And only gradually, like a warmth,

it came to me that the dead don't remain apart
from the living, but after vanishing return as light,
distilled of old hungers, angers and joys. I felt them

close then. Mother. Father. Sister. Three
in brightness on the street. Each as lovely and
distinguished as a single tree shading the parkway.

Yes, they return to us. But only ever as light.
No longer caring as they once did, as we still do
for them. Yet somehow, freed themselves,

freeing us. Or so I felt, as time thickened again
and shimmers on the street began to fade.
They were gone for good. They light my way.

The Wild Turkey

They prefer a field's clean edge for feeding
        or mowed roadside strips with an open view
for spotting predators, foxes mostly
        in New England, now my part of the world.
I knew less of them a year ago
        this winter, walking the woods minutes
before a snow. Brown, gray and black hung
        cold December colors. Brown, gray and black
stood the wild turkey, feeding at a turn
        in the trail. Her feathers lay over feathers
like shingles or armor, but ruffled
        to life as her head lifted, turning my way.
Above a long neck wary eyes rounded,
        wild at the sight of me. Stones, bare trees
and brush surrounded us. Leaf-mold reddened
        the narrow trail. And though neither of us
existed anywhere but where we stood,
        I wished it otherwise ... that winter being
hard time for me, walking off years
        that demanded too much, that played and
replayed their pointless-seeming mysteries,
        as if teaching me to know by not knowing.
Suddenly the turkey opened enormous wings.
        They snapped frighteningly as she rose up,
more jumping than flying. High in a pine
        she roosted, wings folded, her discerning
animal eyes looking down. She was safe, whole.
        Aren't we always so without knowing it,
she seemed to ask. Yet my questions went on.

What must I make of today, tomorrow?
For family, how best should I love and serve
without losing the beat of myself?
Endless human questions. A wild turkey
for answers. And air pressure building,
as if God waited impatiently, irritably,
for me to do the next right thing.
Then a fine, forgiving snow began to fall.

Acknowledgements

I gratefully acknowledge the editors of the following publications in which these poems, sometimes in different forms, first appeared.

The Threepenny Review, "Polk Street"
Alaska Quarterly Review, "House"
Los Angeles Review, "A Few Minutes After Nine"
Willow Review and *Writers Almanac,* "Crying Man"
New Haven Review, "The Polishings" and "Spent"
Spillway, "His Hands."
Writers Almanac, "Mrs. Miller"
Revel, "Mercy," "Spent" and "How to Fold a Wheelchair"
Leon Literary Review, "Carolyn"

For their critical suggestions, teachings and moral support, I'm grateful to David Baker, Alan Shapiro, Martha Rhodes, Maurice Manning, Dan Tobin, Alan Williamson, Baron Wormser, Tyler Mills, and Troy Jollimore.
For her wisdom in shaping these poems into a book, special thanks to Gray Jacobik. And much do I owe to that cloud of witnesses, my community of close poet-friends — especially Jay Brecker, Brian Cochran, Michael Mark and Cintia Santana — and to the places where we met and wrote: Olympic Valley, Asheville and Gambier.

Thank you to Peter Campion and Patrick Davis for their faith in these poems and to the outstanding staff at Unbound Edition.

And to Julie, where my better days begin and end.

About the Author

Charles Douthat is a poet, retired litigator, and visual artist. Born and educated in California, he practiced law for many years in New Haven and began writing poems during a long mid-life illness. His first collection, *Blue for Oceans,* received the PEN New England Award, as the best book of poetry published that year by a New England writer. J. D. McClatchy called it "a wise and haunted book." Charles lives in Weston, Connecticut, with his wife, the artist Julie Leff.

About the Type and Paper

Designed by Malou Verlomme of the Monotype Studio, Macklin is an elegant, high-contrast typeface. It has been designed purposely for more emotional appeal.

The concept for Macklin began with research on historical material from Britain and Europe dating to the beginning of the 19th century, specifically the work of Vincent Figgins. Verlomme pays respect to Figgins's work with Macklin, but pushes the family to a more contemporary place.

This book is printed on natural Rolland Enviro Book stock. The paper is 100 percent post-consumer sustainable fiber content and is FSC-certified.

Again was designed by Eleanor Safe and Joseph Floresca.

Unbound Edition Press champions honest, original voices. Committed to the power of writers who explore and illuminate the contemporary human condition, we publish collections of poetry, short fiction, and essays. Our publisher and editorial team aim to identify, develop, and defend authors who create thoughtfully challenging work which may not find a home with mainstream publishers. We are guided by a mission to respect and elevate emerging, under-appreciated, and marginalized authors, with a strong commitment to advancing LGBTQ+ and BIPOC voices. We are honored to make meaningful contributions to the literary arts by publishing their work.

unboundedition.com